This is a seed. Seeds can have different colors and textures. Some seeds grow into flowers or trees. Some seeds are grains like corn or wheat.

This seed may become a flower.
First, the seed must sprout. To *sprout*
means to "start growing."

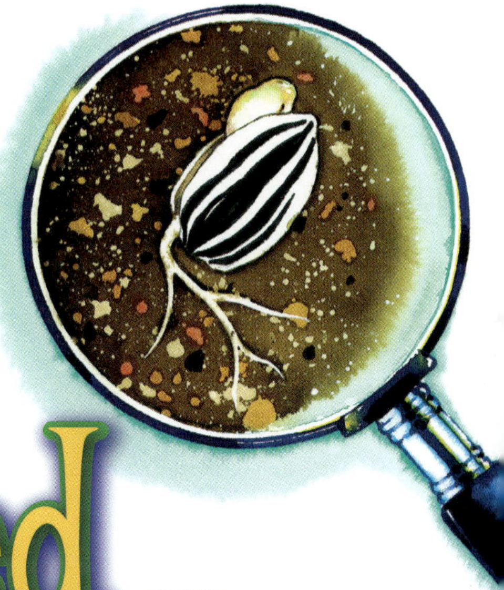

A Seed Sprouts

by Holly Schroeder
illustrated by Denny Bond

Scott Foresman
is an imprint of

Glenview, Illinois • Boston, Massachusetts • Mesa, Arizona
Shoreview, Minnesota • Upper Saddle River, New Jersey

Illustrations
Denny Bond

ISBN 13: 978-0-328-39392-3
ISBN 10:   0-328-39392-4

This is soil. Soil is a material
that plants need to grow. Seeds
sprout in soil.

Seeds need different substances.
Seeds will not grow without water.
Water seeps through the soil to the seed.

This is a root. Roots keep the plant in the soil. Roots bring water and healthy particles to the plant.

This is a seedling. Seedlings grow out of the seed. It will grow toward the sun.

The seedling grows. The plant turns green.

This is a flower. Soil, water, and sun help the plant grow. Then a flower opens, or blooms.

The flower drops seeds onto
the ground. Some seeds will grow
into new flowers.

Follow the diagram that shows the
seed being planted. What do you think
happens next?